FUTURE SYSTEMS

FOR INSPIRATION ONLY

D0794691

FOR INSPIRATION

# ONLY

FOR ME THE SOURCES O

HAUSTIBLE. I DESIGN WIT

AND FOR YEARS I HAVE REA

WITH ADVERTISING AND WHA

BEST SOURCE OF VISUAL I

MAGAZINES, NOT FOR IMAGE

TERESTING OBJECTS, PRO

PEOPLE, PLANTS AND ANIMAL

THAT JUMPS FROM ONE REA

FORM AND PURPOSE FROM DI

IS AN IMPORTANT ROLE O

ACKNOWLEDGE IT. PERHAPS T

HAVE TO HAVE LIVED WITHOU

LIVED IN AN IMAGE CASCAD

WAS NOT THE CASE. WHEN

KIA I WAS SENT SOME COPIE

ISUAL INSPIRATION ARE INEX-
EFERENCE IMAGES IN MIND
IAGAZINES WHICH, ALONG
SEE AROUND ME, ARE THE
GERY. I SEARCH THROUGH
F BUILDINGS SO MUCH AS IN-
SSES, NATURAL PHENOMENA,
HAT CONVEY A MEANING
TY TO ANOTHER, LINKING
ERENT WORLDS. I THINK THIS
IAGAZINES BUT FEW PEOPLE
EE HOW IMPORTANT IT IS YOU
T; MOST PEOPLE TODAY HAVE
INCE BIRTH. FOR ME THIS
VAS YOUNG IN CZECHOSLOVA-
F *LIFE* MAGAZINE FROM

AMERICA. THEY WERE COMP
LIFE. I STILL POSSESS SOME O

IN OUR WORLD THE SOURCE
LIMITLESS. TODAY I SUBSCRIB
THAT DEAL WITH ARCHITE
NEERING, NATURE, LIFE, TH
FIELDS AS POSSIBLE. THIS I
FROM THE PLANETS IN OUTE
EST STRUCTURE OF SUB
EVERYWHERE I FIND TH
RARE AND HENCE, MUST B
STRIKE THE EYE. FOR ME, TH
FROM THE SHAPES, COLOURS
WHICH REVEAL BEAUTY, UGL
NEED OR TRAGEDY.

ATIONS OF ANOTHER WAY OF
HE IMAGES.

F VISUAL INSPIRATION ARE
O OVER TWENTY MAGAZINES
URE, DESIGN, SCIENCE, ENGI-
NVIRONMENT . . . AS MANY
HE WORLD AS WE ALL SEE IT,
PACE DOWN TO THE SMALL-
OMIC PARTICLES ON EARTH.
HARPEST MEANINGS ARE
AVED AS SOON AS THEY
TRONGEST MEANINGS COME
EXTURES AND CONTRASTS
ESS, INGENUITY, HAPPINESS,

*FOR INSPIRATION ONLY* IS M
HUNDRED IMAGES FROM
ASSEMBLED OVER MORE THA
HERE IS ONE THAT TOLD M
SAW IT. EVERY ONE TOUCHE
TRIGGERED MY THOUGHT
REVELATION OF A SHAPE OR
NEED THAT WILL STAY IN M
SYSTEMS SLIDE COLLECTIONS
CREATES AN OPPORTUNITY T
TION OF THIS KIND IS THE ONL
IMMEDIATE BUT ALSO LONG
SPOKEN OR WRITTEN WORD
HAS VERY FEW WORDS.
THE LANGUAGE OF THINGS
IDEAS THAT ARE DRAWN, I

WN SELECTION OF ONE
ARGE COLLECTION I HAVE
WENTY YEARS. EVERY IMAGE
OMETHING THE MOMENT I
NERVE AND THAT WAY
NTO CRYSTALLISATION, A
UNCTION, A METHOD OR A
IND AND IN THE FUTURE
NTIL THE COURSE OF EVENTS
SE IT. I THINK COMMUNICA-
IND IMAGES CAN MAKE. IT IS
ASTING, AND IT NEEDS NO
O GO WITH IT. SO THIS BOOK
ANTED IT TO BE WRITTEN IN
BJECTS, PROCESSES AND
ENTED OR PHOTOGRAPHED,

**THEN REPRODUCED IN PUBLIC**

**IN OUR WORLD MANY IMAGE**
**IN THIS WAY, EVERY MINUTE O**
**EVEN MILLIONS OF COPIES O**
**THOUSANDS, EVEN MILLION**
**TIME CONSIST OF IMAGES. FO**
**REINFORCES THIS COLOURFU**
**ANOTHER MEMORY IS MY FIRS**
**THE SHOCK OF SEEING A BI**
**THE FIRST TIME (SUCH THING**
**CZECHOSLOVAKIA); PERHAP**
**REALLY LEFT ME.**

**NOT EVERYBODY RECOGNISE**
**A WAY THAT CAN BE ORGA**

IONS OR MOVING PICTURES.

F EVERY KIND ARE PUBLISHED
VERY DAY. THOUSANDS, OR
MAGES ARE CIRCULATED:
F SECONDS OF TELEVISION
IE ADVERTISING FORCES AND
MAGE CASCADE AS WELL.
ISIT TO LONDON. I RECALL
DVERTISING HOARDING FOR
VERE UNKNOWN IN 1960s
HAT SHOCK HAS NEVER

HE IMAGES AROUND THEM IN
SED OR USED. NOT MANY

PEOPLE EXPLORE THE REASO
INTERESTS THEM IN A CO
MORE PEOPLE SHOULD NOTIC
TRY TO RELATE TO THEM. WHE
TURAL ASSOCIATION I ALWAY
LOOK AROUND YOU! GET O
BUS AND LOOK DOWN; SEE TH
DOOR OF THE VAN, SEE TH
ADVERTISING HOARDING, LOO
IMAGINE HOW YOU CAN BRIN

WITH IMAGES WE SEE EXCITIN
WHERE, NOT ONLY ON TH
A TRAILER HOME IN THE AME
PERFECTLY FRIED EGG, A PA
PLYWOOD, A VICTORIAN GREE

HY THE IMAGE CASCADE
TRUCTIVE WAY. PERHAPS
HEIR SURROUNDINGS AND
TAUGHT AT THE ARCHITEC-
OLD MY STUDENTS, LEARN TO
HE TOP DECK OF A LONDON
ETAILING OF THE SLIDING
ASH OF COLOUR FROM THE
T ALL THAT YOU SEE AND
TO BEAUTIFY ARCHITECTURE.

HINGS HAPPENING EVERY-
RAWING BOARD. WHEN I SEE
AN WEST, A SEASHELL, A
ICULAR IMAGE OF A SHEET OF
OUSE, A SPACECRAFT OR A

WHEELBARROW BEING USED A
ARE NOT UGLY. I THINK OF AL
OF ALL THE BEAUTIFUL THING
OF THE PRODUCTS WE USE, T
WELDERS, THE PHOTOVOLTAI
THE    HIGH    PERFORMANC
WORK OF ENGINEERS, DESIG
IT IS NATURE, IT IS LIFE – IT I

CHAIR, I SEE THINGS THAT
HE ANONYMOUS DESIGNERS
OUR WORLD, THE MAKERS
HERMOGRAPHS, THE ROBOT
ELLS, THE SOLAR PANELS,
PORTS EQUIPMENT, ALL THE
S, PEOPLE WITHOUT TITLES.
OD.

*JAN KAPLICKY*, 1996

# FUTURE SYSTEMS    PROJECTS

**FUTURE SYSTEMS** IS SYNONYMOUS WITH
ARCHITECTURALLY PIONEERING AND TECHNO-
LOGICALLY CREATIVE DESIGN. THE POTENTIAL
FOR ANONYMITY BEHIND THIS NAME MARKS A
DELIBERATE ATTEMPT TO SACRIFICE PERSON-
ALITIES – IN THIS CASE JAN KAPLICKY AND
AMANDA LEVETE – IN FAVOUR OF A RECOGNISABLE
THEORY AND APPROACH TO ARCHITECTURE. EACH
**FUTURE SYSTEMS** PROJECT, WHETHER IT BE
A CHAMPAGNE BUCKET, A SHELTER FOR THIRD
WORLD DISASTER AREAS, A PRIVATE HOUSE OR
A MEDIA CENTRE FOR LORD'S CRICKET GROUND,
IS BOTH AN EXPLORATION AND AN EXPRESSION
OF THREE-DIMENSIONALITY, CHALLENGING
TRADITIONAL PRECONCEPTIONS OF SPACE.

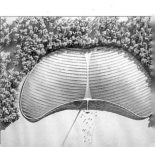

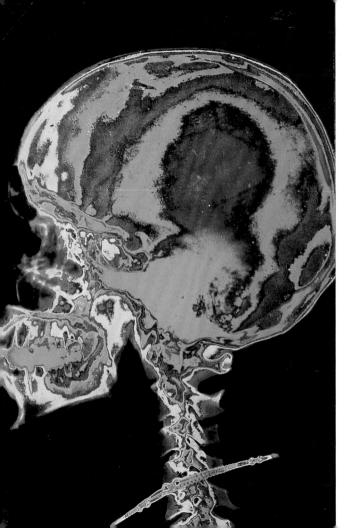

COMPLEXITY
FULLY
EXPOSED

X-RAY

WOMAN'S HEAD

ARTIFICIAL

HEART, 1985

GALLARUS ORATORY, IRELAND, 900AD

**DESIGNER DID NOT GO TO ARCHITECTURAL SCHOOL**

TERMITE HILL, ERONGO MOUNTAINS, SOUTH AFRICA·

**FIRST GREEN BUILDING**

# TOTALLY
# MINIMUM
# SPACE

SUBMARINE BUNK

ROOM,

*USS*

*PORTSMOUTH,*

1980

*HINDENBURG* AIRSHIP DINING ROOM, 1936

# WALKING SLOWLY 200M ABOVE GROUND

NASA MARS LANDING VEHICLE, 1988

**NEW GENERATION OF SPACE RESEARCH**

# START OF A
# BRILLIANT
# IDEA

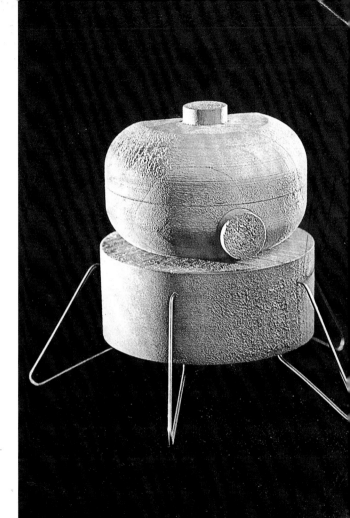

LUNAR MODULE –
FIRST MODEL,
1962

# TWO HEARTS
# ONE SOUL

# MAN OF THE
# FUTURE

NASA AX5 SPACE
SUIT, 1984

NASA SPACE SHUTTLE PARACHUTE, 1979

# SPACE WITHOUT EIGHT CORNERS

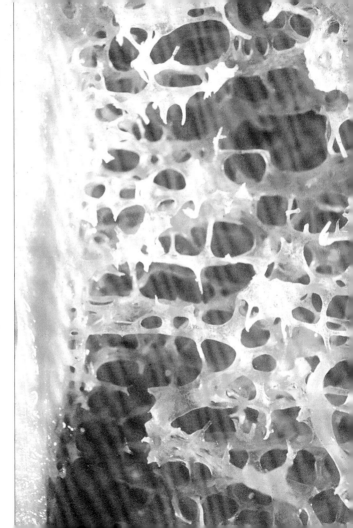

SUCH A
SOPHISTICATION

SPINAL BONE

TISSUE

EGG MASS OF THE SEA SLUG, RED SEA

**SOFT AND TRANSLUCENT**

# 50 YEARS
# AHEAD OF
# ITS TIME

NORTHROP XB-31

BOMBER, 1946

RED SPONGE, RED SEA

**SHAPE OF THINGS TO COME**

*LUCKY LIPS* SEATING, SALVADOR DALI

# MORE SCULPTURE THAN FURNITURE

CARDBOARD HOUSE, NEW YORK, 1991

**MINIMAL RESOURCES**

SHELTER, AFRICA, 1985

**MORE SENSE THAN MANY**

**TIMELESS,
ALMOST
CLASSIC**

PALM HOUSE, BICTON GARDENS, BUDLEIGH, SALTERTON, DEVON
1843

**WHAT A SHAPE AND SPACE INSIDE**

JAGUAR XJ220 *WOODEN BUCK*, 1988

**FIRST 10 ENTIRELY MADE BY HAND**

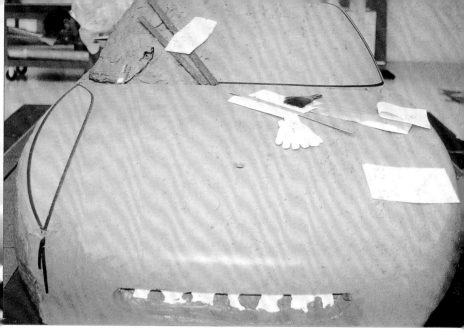

POLYSTYRENE AND CLAY CAR – MOCK-UP

# COMPUTERS WILL NEVER REPLACE MOCK-UPS

41

LOCKHEED F117 WOODEN MOCK-UP, 1985

**ESSENTIAL DESIGN TOOL**

NORTHROP B-2 STEALTH BOMBER, 1989

# NEW SHAPE DICTATED BY NEW REQUIREMENTS

*USS LEXINGTON* AIRCRAFT CARRIER DECK HOOK, 1944

**ARCHITECTURE MAGAZINES WOULD NOT APPROVE**

DE HAVILLAND 'MOSQUITO' BOMBER, 1940

**PLYWOOD AT ITS BEST**

MITSUBISHI HIGH SPEED RESEARCH VEHICLE, 1987

**YOU CAN DRIVE IT COMFORTABLY AT 300KM/HR**

ONLY THE
HUMAN BODY
CAN
COMPETE

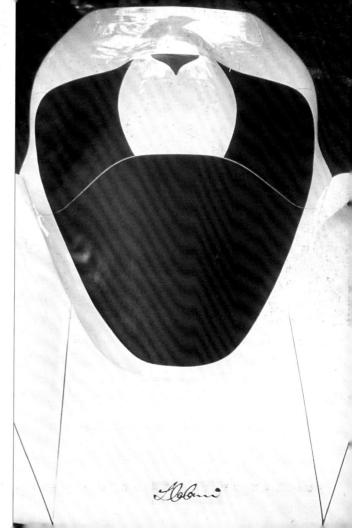

. COLANI GT90
LE MANS' 82 –
CAR, 1965

7

BOEING 747 JUMBO JET, 1969

**CERTAINLY NOT INFLUENCED BY LATEST STYLE**

FUSELAGE INSULATION, 1975

JUST BEFORE DECORATORS COME IN

WILLIS 'JEEP', GENERAL PURPOSE VEHICLE

**NO STYLIST INVOLVED**

KUBELWAGEN TYPE 82, 1940

**TRUE UTILITY**

MOTOR YACHT SUPERSTRUCTURE, 1984

# ALUMINIUM STRUCTURE AT ITS BEST

AIRSTREAM CARAVAN, 1945

**BODYWORK LESS THAN 100KGS**

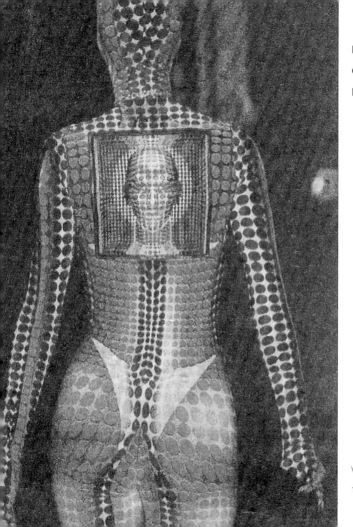

# INDICATION
# OF THE
# FUTURE

VERSACE DRESS,

1995

# ASTONISHING
# BEAUTY

VENUS FIGURE –
DOLNI
VESTONICE,
23,000BC

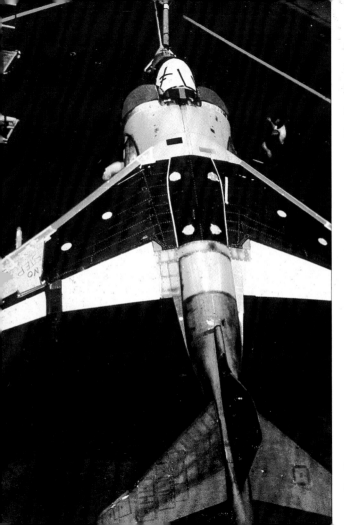

**ONLY PAINT
UNITES
SELECTION
OF
MATERIALS**

HAWKER-SIDDLEY

HARRIER GR

5 6

SPACE SHUTTLE *COLUMBIA*, 1979

**PROTECTION IS MAIN DESIGN CRITERIA**

**STRENGTH,
POWER AND
BEAUTY**

WEIGHT,
WEIGHT,
WEIGHT

GOSSAMER
ALBATROSS,
WEIGHT 96KG,
1978

DOUGLAS DC-3 'DAKOTA', 1935

# SKIN, SPAR AND RIBS WORK TOGETHER – SEMI-MONOCOQUE

CROSSING
OF
EXTRAORDINARY
ELEGANCE

LASKA
IPELINE, 1975

3

AUTOBAHN TUNNEL ENTRANCE, 1970

**ELEGANT INTERVENTION TO LANDSCAPE**

FILM *2001*, 1968

# CONVINCINGLY PREDICTING THE FUTURE

HUMAN BRIDGE

**TOTALLY FLEXIBLE**

WHEELBARROW CHAIR

MORE COMFORTABLE THAN MOST FURNITURE

SCULPTURE,
PAINTING OR
JUST
MODERN
LANDSCAPE?

EVAPORATION
SPIRAL, EL
CARACOL,
MEXICO

WHITE HORSE HILL, UFFINGTON, BERKSHIRE, ENGLAND,
DATE UNKNOWN

THEY HAD SUCH VISION

69

EGG YOLK

**EXQUISITE SHAPE – PERFECT FORM**

DRINKING WATER TANK, KRALIGEN, HOLLAND, 1973

**SHAPE AND STRUCTURE DICTATED BY PURPOSE**

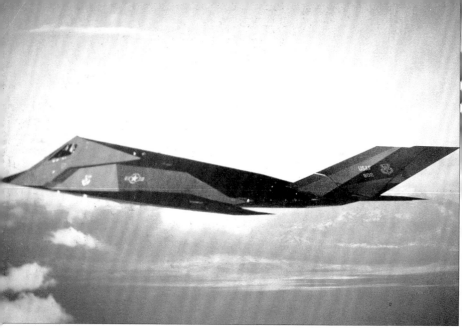

LOCKHEED F117 STEALTH FIGHTER, 1977

**NEW AESTHETIC**

OCKHEED 'ORION' 9C, USA, 1932

FIRST SEMI-MONOCOQUE AEROPLANE

3

SPIDER'S WEB

**LIGHT AND STRONG**

SCHLAICH BERGEMANN DOME, HAMBURG, 1989

**TRULY FLEXIBLE THREE-DIMENSIONAL ROOF STRUCTURE**

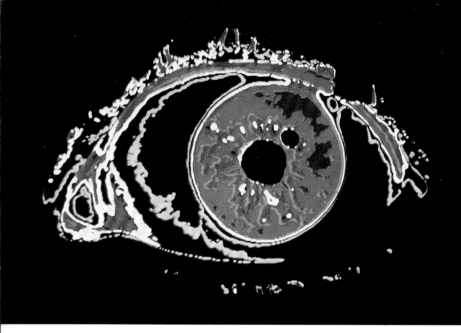

HUMAN EYE

**BEGINNING OF IT ALL**

FREE-SWIMMING JELLYFISH, NW ATLANTIC

# BUILDING IN PLAN

INVISIBLE,
GREEN,
NATURAL
SOURCE OF
ENERGY

UNDERWATER
TURBINE, 1981

7 8

STRENGTH,
SHAPE,
COLOUR

*FUSINUS*
*ANGULATUS* –
*LIGHTFOOT* –
*BONE STRUCTURE*

9

LIVING QUARTERS, INDIA, 1981

**NEVER FEATURED IN ARCHITECTURAL MAGAZINES**

GOLDEN GATE BRIDGE, 1933

BEAUTIFUL BRIDGE, BEAUTIFUL DETAILING,
SILVER PAINT

81

**BEAUTIFUL
AND
ELEGANT
OBJECT
FROM NEW
MATERIALS**

ESA SPACE
RIGIDISED
INFLATABLE
ANTENNA, 1987

NASA 200,000 WATT WINDMILL GENERATOR – 60M DIAMETER, 1979

POWERFUL AND BEAUTIFUL FREE ENERGY
SOURCE

3

ARCO SOLAR CELLS POWER PLANT, HESPERIA, CALIFORNIA, 1982

**POWER OF THE SUN**

EST BED CONCENTRATORS, EDUARDS, CALIFORNIA, 1978

ESSENTIAL PART OF FUTURE BUILDINGS

LOCKHEED C-2 GALAXY RAMP, 1968

**DETAILING CERTAINLY NOT BY ARCHITECTS**

DUESENBERG SJ CAR, 1936

CAN DETAILING EVER BE MORE SOPHISTICATED?

THIS
INFLUENCED
A WHOLE
GENERATION
OF
ARCHITECTS

ATLANTIC WALL,
FRANCE, 1944

SKODA ARMOURED CAR OA VZ 25, 1925

ORGANIC SHAPE FOR UTILITARIAN REASONS

LOCKHEED U-2 PLANE, 1955

**BLACK IS CERTAINLY BEAUTIFUL**

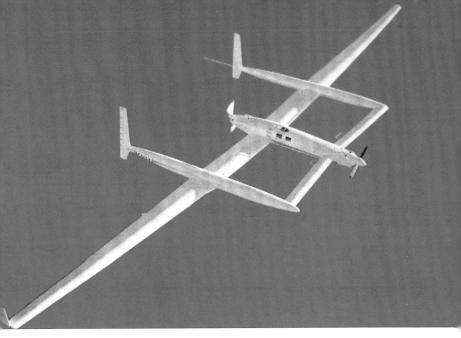

VOYAGER PLANE, 1984

9 DAYS AROUND THE WORLD — DETERMINATION

91

WHAT A
UNIQUE
FORM

ELEGANCE,
SIMPLICITY,
BEAUTY
THAT WILL
LAST

PAIGIO P180
AVANTI PLANE,
1988

**9 3**

SACREMENTO RIBBON BRIDGE, SPAN 127M, 1989

## ANCIENT PRINCIPLE REDISCOVERED

GERMAN MC 30 PONTOON BRIDGE, 1975

DESIGN WITHOUT DESIGNERS

SHAPE,
MATERIAL,
CUT –
ELEGANCE

ISSEY MIYAKE –
BIRD'S BEAK
COAT, 1987

ESSENTIAL
IN A FEW
YEARS TIME

TOP FASHION,
1979

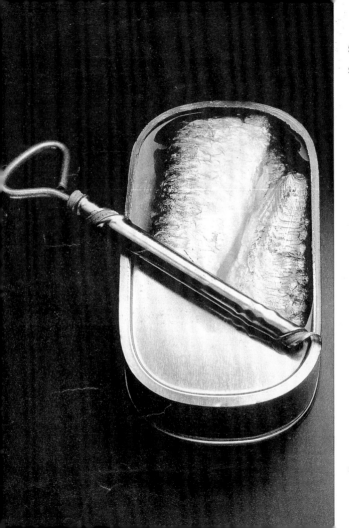

SARDINE TIN,

1824

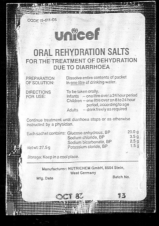

UNICEF LIFE-SAVING PACKAGE, 1980

**SAVES 20,000 CHILDREN'S LIVES A DAY**

99

LEICA CAMERAS, 1913-54

**TRULY UTILITARIAN DESIGN**

Skylab Food Heating/
Serving Tray

NASA 'SKYLAB' FOOD HEATING SERVING TRAY, 1981

**YOU CAN EAT UPSIDE DOWN**

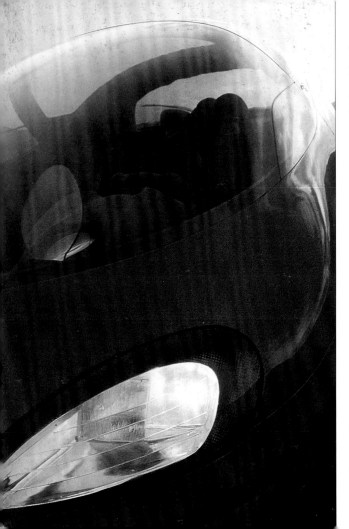

**WHEN WILL
BUILDINGS
ACHIEVE
THIS?**

RENAULT

RACCOON

CONCEPT CAR,

1993

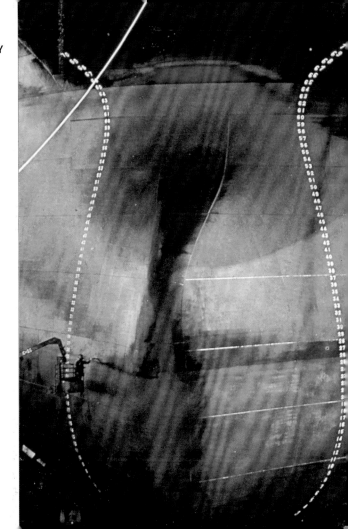

**SCIENTIFICALLY**
**DESIGNED**
**STEEL FORM**

SUPERTANKER

BOW, 1975

**103**

WE STILL
CAN'T BUILD
BUILDINGS
LIKE THIS

*AUSTRALIA II*,
ALUMINIUM
YACHT, 1983

WILL
BUILDINGS
LOOK LIKE
THIS?

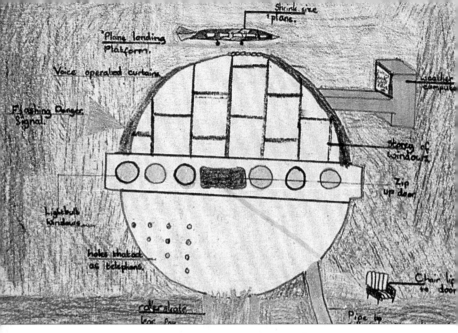

Shrink size plane.

Plane landing Platform.

Voice operated curtains.

Flashing Danger Signal.

weather computer

storey of windows.

Zip up door

Lightbulb windows.

holes that act as telephones.

Chair lip to door.

Pipe in

coke skate lens box.

CHILD'S DRAWING, 1980

TOTALLY SUITABLE HOUSE FOR THE YEAR 2004

IT IS
BEAUTIFUL
EVEN FROM
THE BACK

DONEY 14" TV
SET, ITALY, 1962

**BEAUTIFUL
STRUCTURE,
OBSOLETE
PRINCIPLE**

TRANSPORT
BRIDGE
NEWPORT, NEW
HAVEN,
ENGLAND, 1911

COMPLETE
TRANSFORMATION

SCAFFOLDING ON
ST TYN CHURCH,
PRAGUE, 1986

09

*ENDEAVOUR* J-CLASS YACHT, 1934

**HARMONY OF SHAPE AND NATURE**

*SS SEA SHADOW* STEALTH SHIP, 1986

**EW REASONS, COMPLETELY NEW FORM**

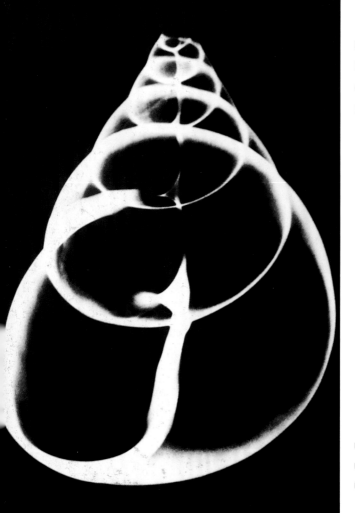

PAPUINA
PULCHERINA
RADIOGRAPH

DETAILING
FOR
HIGHEST
SPEEDS

GMC CC KW 353 TRUCK, 1941

**UTILITY AND SIMPLICITY, CERTAINLY NO STYLING**

ATRA 87, 1935

NSPIRATION FOR MANY YEARS AFTER

ARC DE TRIOMPHE TRICOLOR, PARIS, 1987

**COLOURFUL TRANSFORMATION**

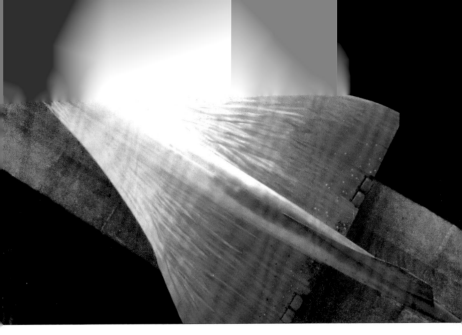

BAC/SUD AVIATION 'CONCORD', 1969

## STUNNING COLOUR SCHEME

TREE HOUSE,

PILA,

SWITZERLAND

**118**

TOTALLY
RELYING ON
QUALITY OF
MATERIALS

SIKORSKY S-64 *SKYCRANE* HELICOPTER, 1965

**TRUE PIONEER IN FUTURE TRANSPORT**

ROBOT CAR BUILDER, 1985

ONE DAY HOUSES WILL BE BUILT THE SAME WAY

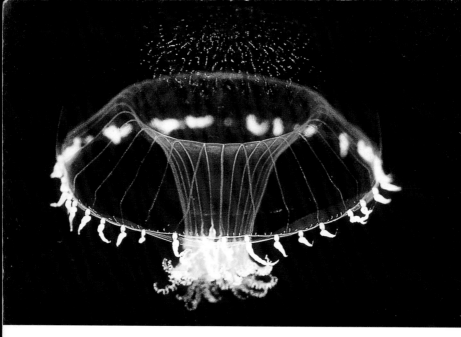

JELLYFISH

**BUILDING OF THE FUTURE**

IMMATIC IRRIGATION SYSTEM, 1985

ONGEST MULTI-FUNCTIONAL TRUSS

BUGATTI TYPE 37, 1929

**ALMOST SCULPTURE**

UGATTI TYPE 51, 1931

ASTONISHING SENSE FOR BEAUTIFUL DETAILS

FIRST PUBLISHED IN GREAT BRITAIN IN 1996 BY
ACADEMY EDITIONS
AN IMPRINT OF

ACADEMY GROUP LTD
42 LEINSTER GARDENS, LONDON W2 3AN
MEMBER OF THE VCH PUBLISHING GROUP

ISBN  1 85490 478 7

DISTRIBUTED TO THE TRADE IN THE UNITED STATES OF AMERICA BY
NATIONAL BOOK NETWORK, INC
4720 BOSTON WAY, LANHAM, MARYLAND 20706

PRINTED AND BOUND IN SINGAPORE